pottery barn kids

kids' rooms

text
margaret sabo wills

photography
melanie acevedo

styling
david benrud

executive editor
clay ide

general editor
gretchen clark

POTTERY BARN KIDS

President Laura Alber

Senior Vice President, General Merchandising Manager Sandra Stangl

Senior Vice President, Creative Services Clay Ide

Vice President, Creative Services Gretchen Clark

Editor Samantha Moss

WELDON OWEN INC.

CEO, President Terry Newell

Vice President, Publisher Roger Shaw

Vice President, Sales and New Business Development Amy Kaneko

Executive Editor Elizabeth Dougherty

Creative Director Kelly Booth

Designer Meghan Hildebrand

Production Director Chris Hemesath

Production Manager Michelle Duggan

Color Manager Teri Bell

First printed 2005. Thanks to Rebecca Poole Forée,
Publisher; Colin Wheatland, Art Director; Jennifer
Block Martin, Managing Editor; Lisa Milestone, Senior
Designer; Maria Behan, Project Editor; and Elizabeth
Lazich, Photo Coordinator.

Pottery Barn Kids: Kids' Rooms was conceived and
produced by Weldon Owen Inc.
415 Jackson Street, San Francisco, CA 94111
in collaboration with Pottery Barn Kids
3250 Van Ness Avenue, San Francisco, CA 94109

Printed in China by 1010 Printing.

10 9 8 7 6 5 4 3 2 1

Library of Congress Control Number 2005926870

ISBN 978-1-61628-145-8

contents

The child-friendly home

As we've both learned firsthand, children instantly transform a home. These changes extend far beyond just the bedroom, because so much of daily life with kids takes place in the playroom, kitchen, bath, and outdoors. A truly nurturing home is one in which every space is unique and inspiring, integrating safety and comfort with a parent's wish for style.

As mothers, our experience has shown us that when it comes to decorating kids' spaces, ease is key. Yet when we looked for realistic ways to bring creativity to our own homes, what we found was surprisingly limited. We published this book so that other parents can learn, as we did, that it doesn't have to be difficult to create beautiful, kid-friendly homes that give our children room to play, learn, and thrive.

Laura Alber
President

Sandra Stangl
Senior Vice President, General Merchandising Manager

spaces for kids

Designing with children in mind

Why do we remember the places of our childhood so vividly? Perhaps it's because first impressions are the strongest, and from a child's perspective, everything is new. Children explore the textures, tastes, smells, sounds, and mysterious workings of the here and now – sometimes adding vibrant splashes of color from their inner imaginative world.

When it comes to their homes, kids relish the familiar, with just a hint of novelty thrown in. Children's bedrooms and playrooms are especially good places to get creative. Involve kids in parts of the planning process, too, which will give them a chance to see their ideas develop into realities. Not that any design is set in stone: your home will evolve as your child grows, keeping pace with his expanding abilities and developing interests. When planning your child's bedroom, begin with a graceful floor plan, surfaces that are simple to maintain, hardworking furniture, and space-saving storage. Introduce fun details like toys and artworks to create a room that is easy to enjoy and, perhaps someday, a joy to remember.

Creating the perfect bedroom

In addition to sleeping, children use their bedrooms for a host of activities

A comfortable bed and smart clothes storage are essential to good bedroom design. And kids love to stake a claim on their room with their own special stuff. Brainstorm with your child to come up with some fun and practical ideas. For instance, he might appreciate bold dashes of a favorite color, a hidden alcove for reading or playtime, or the chance to have his current craze – be it sports, dinosaurs, or robots – played out on sheets, posters, and shelf displays. Include special places for comforting nighttime rituals, such as an easy chair for curling up with a book or a couple of oversize pillows for quiet bedside conversations and stories. Zeroing in on the additions that mean the most to your child lets you create a space that fits him like a favorite pair of shoes.

Playful details

A lineup of vintage toys adds a vivid accent to dark walls, *above*, and stays neatly arrayed on a high shallow shelf built into the paneled wainscot.

Custom tailored

Children enjoy private nooks, such as a cushioned window seat for reading and gazing out the window, *left*. The handy child-height pegs made from kids' toy blocks are another element that tells your child, "This room's just for you."

Ready for anything

While it serves as a cozy nest at the end of the day, a kid's bedroom also has many other functions: it's a quiet haven for reading, a social center when friends come over, and a comfortable place for active, imaginative play, *right*.

READING LIGHT
A bedside table lamp casts a warm pool of light over two nighttime reading areas, the bed and the denim armchair.

CHEERFUL CHALKBOARD
Using a jigsaw and some colorful chalkboard paint, you can make a fanciful feature that not only adds to the decor, but is a great place to write reminder notes.

THEMATIC BEDDING
As the centerpiece of the room, the bed is a natural place to showcase a kid's interests, such as sports, animals, or cars.

STORAGE SOLUTION
A trundle bed's lower level can hold a generous storage drawer or an extra mattress, ready for company.

KID-FRIENDLY DISPLAYS
It's easy to tack new artwork into a frame, which gives your child the chance to showcase his latest and greatest masterpieces.

CHILD-SIZED BOOKCASE
Low shelves hold books and toys conveniently close to the bed and window seat, allowing your child easy access.

COZY NICHE
A comfortable window seat provides a quiet corner for reading and daydreaming.

VIBRANT RUG
This colorful rug, made of durable looped wool, warms up the look of the room and provides a soft surface for play.

Planning the space

As you tailor the bedroom to your child, think about comfort, safety, and fun

By working with the floor plan of the room you're decorating, you can experiment with design without moving a stick of furniture. Start with a comprehensive drawing, a room-design computer program, or even a quick sketch that includes crucial information, such as the placement of windows, vents, and electrical outlets. As you try different configurations and focus your ideas, don't forget to factor in your child's likely traffic patterns, such as how he makes his way from the bed to the closet to his favorite play areas.

Position the largest furniture pieces first, and then tuck in the smaller accessories. Your child's bed might be placed along a wall to save space, positioned more dynamically on a diagonal, or set up as a divider between a play area and a reading corner. Once the bed visually anchors the room, it will be easier to decide where to place pieces like a desk and an armchair.

When designing your child's room, tap into what you know about his personality and favorite activities

Storage can be targeted to each activity zone in the bedroom, with bookshelves for a reading nook, baskets and cubbies to hold toys in a play area, and a dresser placed near the closet for easy dressing. Plan for safety, too, which includes anchoring tall units like an armoire or a bookshelf to the wall.

Since kids like to be where the action is, plan their bedrooms with some portable storage, such as baskets or wagons, to make it easier to transport their favorite gear to family areas. Small children need to stay close to their parents, so your child's bedroom should be comfortable for you, whether you're there to play a game or to tuck in a sleepy child for the night.

Bedroom checklist

Mix and match the following items according to your child's needs to create the perfect bedroom.

Furniture
- bed
- dresser
- armoire
- nightstand
- desk and chair
- armchair
- bookshelf

Bedding
- comforter and duvet cover
- quilt and/or blankets
- sheet sets
- pillows
- bed skirt

Accessories
- rug
- overhead lighting
- lamp for nightstand
- toy chest
- storage baskets and bins
- shelves
- shades or drapes
- bulletin board or chalkboard
- wall art and frames
- alarm clock
- books
- educational toys

Kid-focused design

Children literally enjoy rooms on several levels. Outfit their spaces with rugs to make sprawling on the floor with toys more comfortable, and a child-sized armchair, *right*, for reading. Artworks and collectibles can be placed high so they're admired, not handled, *far right*.

Furnishing your child's room

The furniture choices you make will determine how a room "feels." Talk with your child to come up with some ideas for the overall look of his bedroom, be it a rustic Western theme, sleek modern lines, or a whimsical storybook motif. Then consider the finish. The warm look of natural wood contrasts well with modern decorative touches and hides fingerprints. White finishes can provide a fresh-looking background for a space that's awash in colors, and bright enameled furniture adds its own rich personality to a room.

Some children graduate from the crib to a toddler bed, while others make the transition directly to the twin- or full-sized bed they'll use for years to come. Fun thematic beds, such as those shaped like race cars or boats, add charm to a room, and once they're outgrown, they can be passed along to an appreciative younger sibling or friend. Kids also enjoy beds that provide a cozy sense of enclosure, such as sleigh beds, genuine four-posters, or even "faux-posters" fashioned from ceiling- or wall-mounted canopies.

To finish the room, add a bedside table, comfortable seating, a desk for older children, and storage options like dressers, toy chests, and bookcases. Personalize with fun details, including artworks, toys, and family photos.

Adding color and texture

Most children will answer readily when asked, "What's your favorite color?" But most won't distinguish among each color's infinite shades – say, between cobalt and robin's-egg blue. To move the color dialogue forward, get your child's reaction to concrete examples, such as pictures of different rooms, a color wheel, or a range of paint samples. If your child likes dark or strong colors, you might satisfy that preference by using his favorite hues as accents in a comforter, drapes, or a single painted wall.

When decorating your child's room, the goal is to create a space that's lively without being overwhelming. Intense, rich colors create interest and drama, while neutrals and soft colors lend a feeling of harmony and balance. And as you decorate, don't forget about the color white, which provides the eye with visual relief and prevents a room from feeling too busy.

Texture also plays into color perceptions: smooth, shiny finishes make hues seem lighter and brighter, while plush, matte surfaces make colors look darker and richer

Combining colors provides endless possibilities. High-contrast combinations, which are energetic and fun, begin with attractive opposites. For instance, you might blend selections from the cool green or blue family with warmer elements from the red or yellow range. If you want to create a room that's soothing and mellow, opt for a low-contrast theme, which means organizing your child's room around a single color, or a couple of closely related hues, ranging from a pale pastel to a bright, saturated shade.

A room's colors come to life with lighting. Cool fluorescent illumination plays up blues and greens, while incandescent bulbs enhance yellows and reds. So try to judge paint and fabric samples you're considering by standing under a light source that's similar to the lighting you'll have in the room at home.

Texture is another prime consideration. Many kids are sensitive to how things feel – as you'll quickly discover if you try putting on your child's shoe over a crinkled sock! Cater to that discerning tactile sense with a bedroom that boasts a mix of textures, from soft flannel sheets to a cuddly chenille throw.

Look and feel
Rich blue walls can be echoed in matching bedding, or contrasted with warm red sheets and blankets, *left*. Bedding doesn't just change the look of a room: it can be a great way to appeal to your child's acute sense of touch. Opt for pleasing textures, such as nubby cotton, *above*.

Making room to grow

When anticipating your child's needs, bear in mind that they'll change as swiftly as he grows. With a bit of ingenuity and planning, though, you can easily adapt a bedroom tailored to an exuberant toddler, *below*, to suit an active school-age child, *right*, and eventually even a preteen. While keeping the same crisp color scheme in creamy white, Prussian blue, and deep red, you can successfully update this bedroom by swapping out a couple of furniture pieces

PLAYFUL CLOSET
In this toddler's room, the closet door is temporarily replaced by a curtain of red canvas for easy access, with roll-up flaps that double as a puppet theater or provide peep holes for a game of hide-and-seek.

KID-HIGH PEGS
A series of pegs made from toy blocks keeps everyday clothing staples within a young child's easy reach.

SOFT ADDITION
This denim-covered ottoman will become a footrest later, but it's just the right size for a toddler's step stool, seat, or play surface.

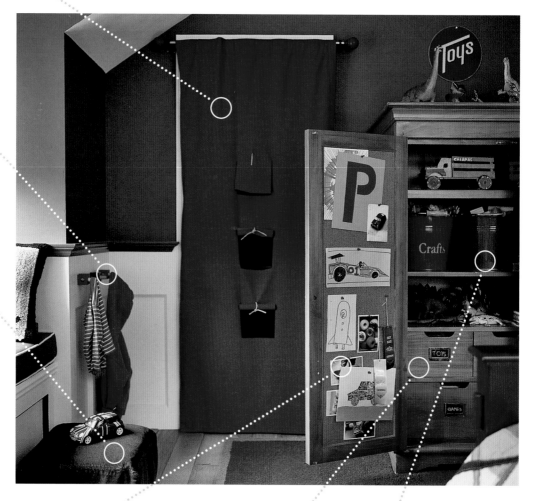

BULLETIN BOARD
The bulletin board built into the armoire door is large enough to display a gallery of favorite artworks and photos.

ARTFUL ARMOIRE
A country-style armoire neatly hides its myriad contents with just one swing of its double doors.

ACCESSIBLE STORAGE
Colorful buckets and low, easy-to-open drawers are perfect for storing a toddler's toys and art supplies.

and adding some age-appropriate details. To plan for the changes ahead, seek out simple, versatile furnishings or classically styled mix-and-match modular units that you can reconfigure for new uses – since the shelves that display storybooks and stuffed animals today may need to hold textbooks and soccer trophies tomorrow. Sometimes, though, it's fun to celebrate the moment, so include a few whimsical pieces scaled just for your child right now.

DISPLAY SPACE
A designated display area can adjust as your child's interests change, shifting from a toddler's toys to a schoolchild's trophies and mementos.

TECH CENTER
Today's children view a computer as both a toy and an essential tool. Adding one requires desk space, as well as storage for discs, manuals, and other related gear.

STUDY AREA
Setting up a study area with reference books and school supplies creates a place where your child can focus quietly on homework.

OPEN SPACE
Rearrange furniture in the rooms of older children to open up more space for larger toys and sports gear.

RETURN OF THE DOOR
The closet now gets more use, so the door, which also has a neater, grown-up look, replaces the curtain.

ON NOTICE
A smaller bulletin board, prominently displayed, holds a school-age child's souvenirs and reminders.

dressing

Getting ready for the day

Watch a toddler breathlessly concentrate on a stubborn button, and you can appreciate the milestone reached in learning to get dressed. This developmental benchmark involves not just fine motor skills and a sense of sequence, but an emerging understanding that "this is me."

Many kids are surprisingly passionate about what they want to wear, perhaps because they attribute some of the magic of dress-up and costumes to daily dressing. Other children are more relaxed about their wardrobes, putting on whatever is handy. But whether your child loves or merely tolerates the idea of clothing, an organized, appealing dressing area, where everything is easy to find and simple to put away, will promote family harmony and help your child master the art of dressing.

Well-planned storage simplifies dressing. While you can stow infrequently worn clothing neatly out of sight, children tend to focus better on open, on-view storage, particularly if you divide the contents into clearly labeled categories. Pegs and racks at a kid-friendly height make it simple to grab an outfit and (let's hope) hang it up at day's end.

RIBBON-SHADE LAMP
Adorned by a cascade of breeze-catching ribbons, the ceiling lamp's shade suggests a colorful bed canopy.

SHEER CURTAINS
Airy fabric panels hung on small rings screen off the open storage spaces in this closetless room.

PATTERN AND TEXTURE
Kids love rich, varied textures in both clothing and furnishings.

CLOTHING AS DECOR
Personalize your child's dressing area – and add some color – by displaying a special outfit.

LABELED SHELVES
Sorting clothes from top to bottom, and labeling each category with a simple picture, can encourage organizational skills. (**See page 36** for more details on this idea.)

FULL-LENGTH MIRROR
A large mirror mounted securely to the wall enhances a room's sense of light and space while serving as a practical checkpoint for assessing the day's outfit.

STORAGE SOLUTIONS
See-through storage bins cue your child on where to find and put back those tiny treasures and small accessories.

COLORFUL CONTAINERS
Keep an eye out for imaginative containers and decorative boxes that provide a visual splash while corralling clutter.

Planning a wardrobe

Let your child help choose a few outfits, then put them on display in her room

Thinking about your child's daily routine can inspire specific design ideas for a dressing area. Many small children, heedless of the clock, lose momentum during the morning launch. Give them a boost with very accessible clothing storage, like rods, pegs, and hooks at comfortable heights, and open storage that provides easy visual clues. Keep the storage streamlined by winnowing out unwanted or outgrown clothing. To minimize last-minute decisions, assemble some outfits for the next few days, right down to the smallest accessories. With your child's help, line up the shoes and clothing in a designated spot to cut down on confusion and the need for extra prompting.

Assembling the pieces
A casual display of your child's clothing, *above*, with its lively colors and details, can double as decoration. And lining up clothes for the days ahead speeds things along during the morning hustle.

Buttons and bows
Choose clothing geared to your child's developing dexterity. Zippers are easier than buttons, and bows are fine if they're already tied, *left*, as most children don't master tying them until they're at least five.

A child-ready dressing area
An improvised clothing rod, *right*, looped in ceiling-hung ribbons, makes garments easy to reach. The adult-sized armoire will serve long past childhood, but is made friendlier with small, door-mounted hooks and ribbon-trimmed mirrors scaled to your child's needs today. Anchor tall furniture pieces securely to the wall.

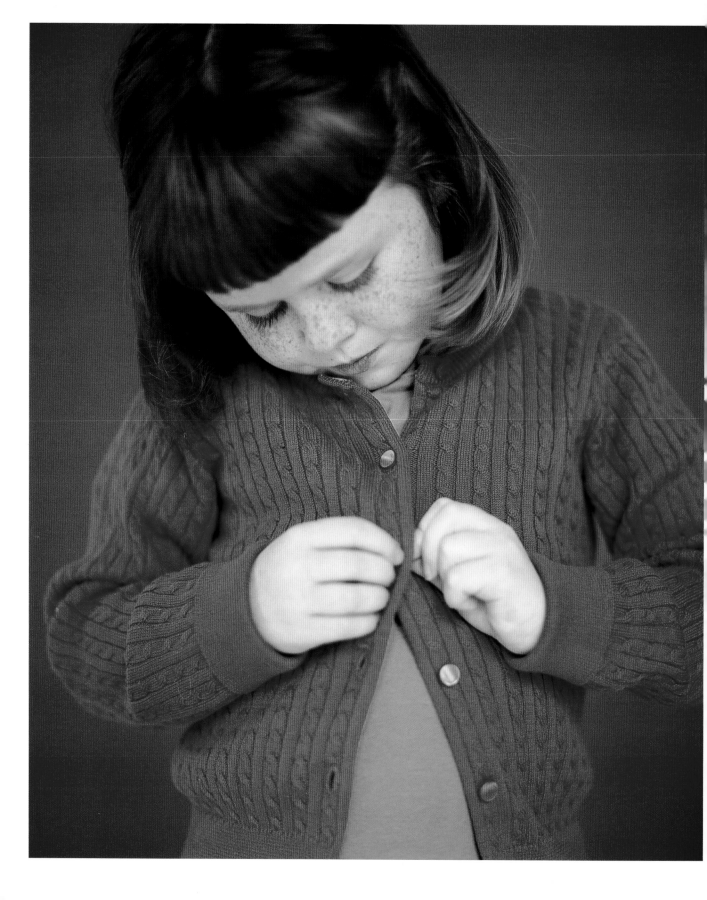

" I'm big now,
and I can dress
all by myself **"**

Categorizing clothes

Top-to-bottom labels

Brightly colored pictures help even a toddler locate clothes.

1 Arrange clothing on shelves by categories, from shoes on up.

2 On stiff cardboard, draw icons of clothes in red-rimmed circles, evoking information signs. Fill the shapes in with markers, or have your child complete the artwork.

3 Apply signs to the shelves with double-sided adhesive tape.

Marking storage areas with pictures shows kids where to stow their stuff

For both adults and kids, good storage means consolidating and containing things into logical categories. A child can understand that it's quicker to find a pair of pants when they're all kept in the same spot. (Make a toddler giggle by saying the shirts stay together to tell shirt stories.) Children are more likely to help themselves if their possessions are stored on view and within easy reach. Coordinated baskets, bins, and boxes can neaten up the contents of versatile open shelves. For an extra cue, put on labels with either written words or simple iconic signs. After you've consolidated the items in a category, divide the clothes into manageable amounts for easier retrieval.

Visible storage
On-view storage tells a child where to find and put back clothes, *right and far right*, especially with the added information of colorful and cheerful pictorial signs.

Pairing left with right

Matching shoes with each other becomes fun for your child if it's part of a game

Because putting on footwear is often the last step in getting your child out the door, keeping shoes organized can head off last-minute scrambles. Any storage solution should be placed either near the point of first use or where shoes tend to get dropped once they're taken off. For instance, you might choose to have your child store some everyday footwear near whichever door she uses most, say, in a front-hall closet.

Shoe racks, bags, or cubbies – or a rolling bin tucked underneath the bed – can offer convenient storage when space is tight. Or, as in this simple-to-create craft project, shoes can be colorfully displayed on a low shelf, where they can be easily spotted and grabbed on the go.

Where the shoe fits
Simple fill-in-the-blank storage templates, *left and far left*, introduce your child to the concept of storing shoes properly by making an enjoyable game of it.

Storing small treasures

Picture-pretty storage

Here's a creative way to keep the small details at eye level.

1 Remove the glass from a picture frame, then paint the border. A neutral white will complement the changing colors of the contents.

2 Remove the insert panel from the frame, and wrap it with a colorful fabric. Secure by using a hot-glue gun to adhere the fabric edges onto the reverse side of the insert.

3 Top the fabric with an assortment of ribbons, hot-gluing both ends of the ribbons onto the back side. Leave slack in the ribbons for clips and pins. Replace the panel in the frame with the ribbons facing out.

4 Hang the frame at child height, preferably near a mirror or dresser, so hair clips, elastics, and pins can be hooked onto the ribbons.

5 Add a couple of hooks at the base of the frame to store larger accessories, *far right*.

Putting on the finishing touches
From choosing their accessories to experimenting with hairstyles, *right*, children enjoy making decisions about their appearance. A beribboned picture frame, *far right*, doubles as an attractive organizer for easily mislaid hair trims.

Organize your child's accessories into displays that add character to a bedroom

Some kids just love – and quickly accumulate – assorted belts, ribbons, jewelry, hair clips, and even stylish socks. Individually, they don't seem like a big storage issue. But these easily misplaced items multiply quickly, causing trouble out of proportion to their size when a search for a favorite accessory brings dressing to a screeching halt.

To round up accessories, sort them according to type and store them in appropriately sized containers or a shallow drawer. You might even jazz up your child's room by turning them into part of the decor. A series of large hooks or a painted tin tray can arrange pint-sized accessories neatly, which also enables your child to find them more easily.

Keeping an eye on the details

To encourage children to pick up their things, use open storage containers that show what goes where

From a child's point of view, opening a door or lifting a lid adds an extra step to storage. Though kids are seldom averse to just leaving things out, they are equally pleased to use smart, one-step open storage to hold their everyday necessities. On-view storage works best when it's divided into compartments. Coordinated bins, baskets, and boxes separate contents and present an attractive, orderly face. See-through wire mesh or clear plastic containers leave it to their contents to provide the colorful decorative touch.

A laundry "shoot"
The lid on the laundry hamper is one more obstacle in the quest to get dirty clothes off the floor and into the washer. This laundry bag's open hoop, *left*, invites a quick toss of clothing, turning cleanup into a sporting challenge.

Tucked away yet on display
Slim bins fronted with clear tilt-out panels, *right*, turn the accessories inside into a colorful display. The bins handily divide a modest vertical space into storage scaled for all those small items.

Teaching your child to dress

Learning to dress independently is one of childhood's rites of passage. Parents can help things along with gentle instruction and appropriate clothes. Most kids begin putting on their own shirts and pants by age two or three, a process made easier by clothes with elastic waists and cuffs. As children grow older, they become deft with zippers, snaps, buttons, and bows.

Fastening feats

Zippers are usually easier for kids to manipulate than buttons (especially if you point out that the zipper tab down at the bottom has its "mouth" open, ready to "bite" onto the other side). Buttons require a bit more coordination, and the small buttons on kids' clothes may be especially challenging. If your child wants to practice her buttoning skills, wrap a chair with an adult cardigan that has large buttons and loose holes, which are easier for small hands to grasp. Then teach her the trick of pushing the button while simultaneously pulling the buttonhole open.

Tips for tying shoelaces

There are numerous ways to teach your child how to tie her shoes. Just type "shoelace tying" into an Internet search engine and you'll find dozens of options. However, it's best to settle on one knot-tying method to share with her (more than one option could be confusing). Several bow-tying methods involve a story, which is a great way to capture a child's attention and help keep the steps in the correct order.

For instance, one favored story is the rabbit tale: "Once there was a field" (tie the basic over-under knot), "and in the middle was a tall tree" (make an upright loop). "A rabbit came and hopped all the way around the tree" ("hop" the loose end of the other lace around the loop). "Then it saw a hole" (point out the hole made by the lace crossing the loop) "and popped in" (poke the middle of the "rabbit" lace through), "but the rabbit's ears still stuck out" (show the loops in a bow).

When teaching the art of tying shoes or even fastening buttons, have your child sit on your lap and bring your arms around her so she can view the actions from the appropriate perspective.

creating

Nurturing the creative spirit

"It has taken me a whole lifetime to learn to draw like a child," mused Pablo Picasso. Perhaps he admired how kids view the familiar with fresh eyes and eager imaginations, exploring colors and forms without concern for perfection.

It's a magical moment when toddlers first wrap a fist around a crayon and revel in the power to unleash dots, swirls, and colors. As they gain dexterity and a feeling that art should reproduce the real world, preschoolers attach names to their sometimes mysterious scribblings. School-age children strive to make their drawings look like the objects they're portraying. To help kids sustain pleasure in the creative process, don't ask "What is it?" but say "Tell me about what you've made." An open-ended discussion of artwork celebrates the fun of creation, which, after all, is where every artist finds inspiration.

Parents can encourage imaginative explorations by providing children with a warm, comfortable space that's generously outfitted with versatile and age-appropriate art supplies. And practical, washable furniture and floors take the worry out of wonderfully messy crafts.

ARTFUL BUCKETS
Mount buckets of art supplies on low hooks, and kids can reach them easily and carry them to the table as needed.

HANGING PAPER ROLL
With drawing paper mounted low on the wall, young artists can tear off sheets that are perfectly sized for their projects.

CHILD-SIZED SINK
Having running water in the craft corner, or at least nearby, simplifies the cleanup of both child and tools. A decorative canvas skirt conceals cleaning, art, or other supplies.

DROP-CLOTH PROTECTION
Safeguarding the floor with an absorbent plastic-backed painter's drop cloth is a good way to prepare for the spills and splashes of children's artistic endeavors.

TOOLS OF THE TRADE
Ensure that young artists have everything they need to realize their artistic visions, such as paint, paintbrushes, crayons, and chalk.

CHALKBOARD WALL
Make it okay to write on the walls (sometimes) with a rainbow of chalks and a wainscot surfaced in spray-on chalkboard paint. (**See page 59** for details.)

FULLY EQUIPPED TABLE
For a custom-tailored art center, cut down an old kitchen table to child height, finish it with washable enamel, and cut holes in the tabletop for tip-proof storage of art-supply containers. (**See page 56** for details.)

SITTING PRETTY
Child-sized chairs, or adult chairs cut down to size, make kids more comfortable as they create.

Stocking your art room

This kid-friendly craft corner brims with art supplies at the ready

One of the primary pleasures children find in art is the joy of dabbling in different materials. Paper can be newsprint, construction paper, or poster board; paints range from tempera and fingerpaints to acrylics and watercolors; drawing tools include crayons, colored pencils, markers, and chalk. Add in squishy clays, fabrics, glitter, string, stamps, bits of nature, and more.

Simple, flexible storage with open shelves and a range of containers will adapt to such a diverse, ever-changing array of supplies. Store the raw materials in logical categories, and your child will know where to look – especially if open buckets and transparent containers provide visual clues.

The raw materials
By organizing the various papers, scissors, crayons, and other staples of kids' crafts, *above*, you can present your child with an inspiring range of artistic possibilities.

A sink for kids
If your arts-and-crafts area adjoins the appropriate plumbing, you can add a sink at child height, *left*, to make cleanup a breeze. Or the craft area can simply be planned near the kitchen, bath, laundry area, or utility room to give your child convenient access to running water.

Storage and display
Kids' creations and the necessary ingredients, when stored in buckets, boxes, and smooth-edged cans, *right*, add up to an appealing visual jumble. A clothesline with old-fashioned pins can display new works, while portfolio boxes might hold a chosen few as keepsakes.

" I love to draw
scary pictures
for my friends **"**

Customizing a table

Create an inspiring workspace for young artists by looking at it from their perspective

An old table takes on a new role as a perfectly scaled work surface.

1 Cut the table's legs to kid height 22–24" (56–61cm). Cut down the legs of the accompanying chairs or find suitable kids' chairs.

2 Measure your supply containers and cut holes in the tabletop to hold the buckets and cups securely.

3 Clean the table thoroughly of old wax and grease. Apply a primer, followed by a coat of washable semigloss enamel in a neutral color.

When you design a children's art area, you prepare it for free-spirited spills and splashes. Consider making the craft area a sociable spot, with chairs and tabletop space for siblings and friends to work together. With all the ingredients in one place, they will spend less time hunting for supplies, leaving more time for the drawing and painting. As attention spans grow, kids might want to leave out a work-in-progress so they can finish it another day.

Since young kids like to stay close to caregivers, and older ones require some supervision, locate the craft area near your kitchen or office so it's easy to stop by. Supplies kept in buckets can be toted around and scooped up at cleanup time.

Secure storage
Distracted young artists are likely to tip over crayon boxes and tubs of rinse water. This kitchen-table-turned-art-center, *above and right,* secures art supplies with no-tip buckets placed in tabletop openings.

Making chalkboards

Once the surface is readied with special paint, the writing on the wall is good news

When children first start scribbling and watch, fascinated, as marks appear, a wall's vast expanses are awfully tempting. With a stretch of chalkboard in a child's room or an art corner, kids can more acceptably explore the pleasures of creating on such a wondrously wide plane.

Use chalkboard paint, which now comes in a variety of colors, as a bold wall accent and the basis of your child's new "canvas." To convey the idea that this wall alone is the one for free-form artwork, frame the area with molding or washable paint.

Use low-dust chalk and dampened sponges as erasers to minimize clouds. Or create an equally inviting art wall with felt-tipped pens and a dry-erase or plastic-coated board.

Pick a convenient spot on the wall and use a brush-on or spray coating to create a chalkboard.

1 If your wall is uneven, smooth it out with sanding or spackle.

2 Apply a base coat of paint on the frame. Allow it to dry.

3 Mark off the chalkboard area with straight lines of masking or painter's tape. Double-check the straightness of the lines with a level.

4 Apply the chalkboard paint within the outline, following the manufacturer's instructions. Remove tape while the paint is still damp.

5 Add practical extras near the new chalkboard, such as colorful bathroom hooks or furniture knobs for holding buckets of chalk.

A bevy of buckets
Chalkboard paint creates a blank slate for a child's imaginative doodlings, *left*. The chalkboard is even handier when you add hooks to hold bright buckets of chalk and other art supplies, *far left*.

Displaying artwork

Showcase the creative endeavors of your enthusiastic young artist

A large showcase area presents a bright medley of kids' artwork.

1 Block out a gallery wall in an informal area, such as the kitchen or family room. A soft-colored background and plenty of light will enhance the artworks' hues.

2 Install a display system that easily lets you and your child change and add new pieces. One option is long corkboard strips, available from stores that carry office and school supplies. They often come with a peel-and-stick adhesive backing that makes installation quick and simple.

3 Complete the display with bright, oversize pushpins, which will be easily spotted if they fall to the floor.

4 Keep a step stool nearby for the exhibit's curator, your child.

Children love to see work they've made with their own hands put on display, but parents soon realize that the refrigerator door can hold only so much. For a more comprehensive approach, designate a wall as a larger gallery space, so that many pictures can be displayed at once. Parent and child can thin out the collection now and then, picking a special few for framing or storing (perhaps along with a caption that describes the story behind the picture). Other works can be sent to relatives or even used as stationery.

Three-dimensional craft projects require tabletops, shadow boxes, or shelves for display in the child's room and elsewhere. If treasured artworks need to make way for new additions, photograph them and compile the photos in a scrapbook; this can be especially useful for bulky pieces. Some parents and children like to use a system of keepsake boxes, one for each year, to preserve carefully culled artworks and mementos. Flat, lidded, stackable containers can store numerous memories in a space-efficient way.

Picture this
Frames and shadow boxes, *right*, highlight a child's favorite pieces. A casual, easily updated corkboard display, *far right*, presents an ever-changing mix of art in a way that evokes the fun of creation.

Keeping supplies within reach

Children will see fresh possibilities with a bright array of paper, crayons, glitter, and other fun materials

Sometimes kids tackle art projects with clear instructions, specific materials, and parental involvement; at other times they're experimenting on their own with anything that strikes their fancy. Either way, art supplies should be readily accessible to allow your child to get right down to the task at hand. Stackable storage systems with a variety of open cubbyholes provide access that's child high – and you can adapt the setup easily when your budding artist decides to branch out into new frontiers of creativity.

Buckets of fun
Colorful buckets, *left*, and their vibrant contents are great for brightening the decor while keeping art supplies handy.

Smart sorting
Wooden bulk bins, *right*, are an option for storing art materials in a way that's not only tidy, but divides supplies into logical and easily visible categories.

Fostering your child's creativity

Kids have a jump on thinking creatively. Since they don't have many preconceived ideas, they startle us with their fresh observations. They're naturally equipped with a hunger for knowledge, a playful take on language, and an experimental attitude toward art. If you encourage children's natural instincts for inquiry and innovation, they'll hold onto those healthy attitudes as they grow.

All the makings

Part of creativity involves seeing new possibilities – or unexpected connections – in the familiar. If your child enjoys building projects and three-dimensional crafts, he or she might enjoy poking around for ideas in a "bits box." This is simply a large container in which you can toss potential craft materials like cardboard tubes, beads from a broken necklace, brass washers, iridescent wrapping paper, stickers from junk mail, or natural objects picked up on walks. Get out the box on a rainy afternoon so your child can look through it to come up with ideas for exciting new projects.

Open to ideas

Supply and storage needs change as your child explores the visual arts, from two-dimensional works on paper to three-dimensional sculpture, building projects, and crafts. Your child will do many projects on his own, but some kids require parental help with cutting, measuring, or following step-by-step instructions. The extra effort for these more complicated projects pays off, since kids enjoy both the time spent with adults and the chance to see the finished product emerge from the raw materials.

You can encourage your child to explore his artistic range by "commissioning" artwork to fill a display gallery. Simply choose a broad theme that will spark visual ideas and memories from your child's small but expanding range of experiences. Some themes to consider are "Holidays," "Things That Make Me Laugh," "The Five Senses," or "Weather" (with words like "rainy," "sunny," and "snowy" as prompts). Let your child explore the different ideas with various art supplies. To add the finishing touch, suggest that he title his works of art, then help him add labels to his creations. Be sure to put them on display for all to enjoy.

playing

Creating perfect play spaces

Children play wholeheartedly, not just to have fun, but also to learn about the world. Babies and toddlers cherish the chance to explore their surroundings, which should be full of fascinating things to pull, push, prod, and drop. Imagination blossoms by age three or four, a time when kids add layers of make-believe onto daily reality. School-age children are increasingly social and verbal, seeking out more challenging games as well as starting to enjoy the world of sports.

Kids see that we value play when we provide them with free time, our interaction, and age-appropriate playthings. Classic toys – blocks, boxes, clay, and dolls – endure through the generations because they can be endlessly adapted to a child's own storylines.

Create havens for play, be it physical, creative, interactive, or daydreamy. Ideally, a play area will have lots of open space, arts-and-crafts supplies, building sets, and a table and chairs ready for constructing, drawing, writing, and other projects. So let the games begin...

TARGETED LIGHTING
The adjustable cords of these vintage-style ceiling fixtures allow them to be hung at the height that's ideal for the room.

AT CHILD HEIGHT
An oversize schoolhouse clock, brought down to a kid's eye level, marks the hours as they fly by in a spacious yet child-scaled room.

GAMES AT THE READY
Make the tabletop tantalizing by incorporating the playing boards of your child's favorite games. (**See page 76** for details.)

JAM SESSION
Toys stored by category invite imaginative combinations. A collection of musical toys inspires tuneful sessions.

A MULTIPURPOSE TABLE
Balancing out the playroom's open spaces, some tables pushed together (or one large one) accommodate board games, building sets, and crafts.

WONDER WALL
Chalkboard paint can be used to transform any wall into a vast chalkboard (**see page 59** for details), and the addition of a basketball hoop makes it the star attraction of the playroom.

CREATIVE CUBBIES
These stackable wooden bins make it easy to create custom storage to fit any play space.

ACCESSIBLE STORAGE
Colorful open baskets allow you to gather all kinds of toys with a few quick scoops — and hold everything in easy reach.

FUN AND FUNCTIONAL
A floor of durable, easy-to-clean linoleum is a smart idea for a playroom with lots of foot traffic. And a bold checkerboard pattern lends kid-pleasing visual appeal.

READY FOR FRIENDS
Comfortable beanbag chairs welcome buddies during social engagements — or provide a cozy haven for reading and daydreaming in quieter times.

Making room to play

Fun takes many forms, so kids' spaces should accommodate a range of activities

Space permitting, a designated playroom offers great advantages: less clutter in the bedrooms, an assigned home for most of the toys (however far they roam), and a spot for active play and visiting friends. An adaptable play space might mix hard and soft flooring, bright colors, and cheerful lighting. The basic elements are simple: plenty of open space, a durable table ready for any manner of projects, comfortable seating, building sets, art supplies, and lots of games. Tumbling mats, balls, a dance bar, or an exercise area encourage active play, and props such as a raised stage, puppet theater, box of dress-up clothes, or play kitchen spur kids to exercise their imaginations, too.

Energy management
Play can be creative and contemplative, or expansive and hands-on. Providing toys and materials for physical activities geared to the available space, *above*, can make rainy days speed by.

A joyful noise
Keep a corner full of instruments, *left*, to let kids explore the art of sound. If toys are stored in understandable categories at a child-friendly height, kids will know where to go to find what they're looking for (and perhaps even put it back later).

Center of activity
A generously sized table (or a pair of tables) and child-sized chairs, *right*, give kids space for games or creative projects, such as constructing a make-believe city or folding and stringing together a chain of paper airplanes, *top right*.

" When we laugh too hard, I drop the ball "

Keeping it together

Smart storage expands to accommodate toys, games, crafts, and building sets

Board-game tabletop

Colorful game boards, released from their boxes, are spread across a table, inviting play.

1 Choose a child- or adult-sized table suitable for game playing. Arrange a variety of playing boards from favorite games on the tabletop.

2 Cover the boards with a piece of clear acrylic plastic. (Craft or home-improvement stores can cut plastic sheets to fit your table.)

3 Keep game pieces and directions in the original boxes, making sure the boxes are stored in a place that's easy for your child to access.

How can you bring some order to a play area when your child likes to have everything on view – and his toy collection seems to expand every day? A first step is paring it down to the toys he actually uses (perhaps packing away a few outgrown favorites for sentimental reasons).

It might be easy to scoop all your child's playthings into one huge bin, but then he'll likely ignore what's buried in the depths – or dump it all to search for a favorite toy. For more targeted storage, use big bins and chests for bulky toys and house the rest in smaller containers, either shallow, transparent, or clearly labeled. Low shelves and cubbies can hold baskets, plastic tubs, mesh bins, or sturdy cardboard boxes.

Fun central
A long table gives children plenty of room to build, *right,* play games, *far right,* or indulge in a bit of both.

Finding hideaways

Be they simple or lavish, the secret nooks of childhood are the stuff of memories

Perhaps because the world seems so big, kids gravitate toward enclosed, child-sized spaces, whether they're finely crafted playhouses or giant cardboard boxes decorated with crayon drawings. When they're ensconced in a place of their own, children unleash their imaginations and revel in role-playing. They also enjoy discovering the material world of gadgets, proportions, weights, textures, and cause and effect. Sometimes kids want to be on their own, constructing with blocks, card tables, or just blankets. At other times, they're thrilled to work alongside an adult who can show them the magic of using tools like hammers, pulleys, and levels to make construction jobs easier.

Pulley power

To raise supplies up to a lofty spot, use a pulley. Kids will ponder how pulling down makes things go up.

1 Above a deck, balcony, or child's treehouse, securely mount a small hardware-store pulley and thread it with a smooth, strong rope.

2 Secure one end of the rope in the play area; on the rope's other end, tie a clip that's easy to manipulate, such as a carabiner.

3 Show your child how to pull hand over hand to bring up a bucket or basket of goodies like snacks or stuffed animals.

Ruling the roost
A square-timbered treehouse, *far left*, becomes a castle or pirate ship. A pulley for hoisting up treats and treasures, *above and left*, makes the treehouse more fun.

Celebrating the outdoors

Transform tic-tac-toe from a quiet indoor pursuit to a fun outdoor activity by increasing the scale.

1 Cut pegboard to the desired size, or ask the retailer to do it for you. If you have a sandbox or an open toy-storage area, size the board so it can do double duty as a lid.

2 Cover it with latex paint in a lively color and let it dry completely.

3 Mark off a tic-tac-toe grid with masking or painter's tape. Use the rows of holes as a line guide.

4 Paint the background in a vivid tone for a good contrast. Remove the tape before the paint dries.

5 When the pegboard is dry, seal it with a clear, nontoxic coating to make it more weather resistant.

6 Have your child gather stones and sticks (or any other marker he or she likes) for making x's and o's.

Create some outside areas where your child's boundless energy can spill over

Children love to get outside so they can bask in freedom and physical expression. Exterior play areas that are in plain view of your home help you keep tabs on those high spirits. The ideal outdoor play space offers not only sun and shade, but also soft grass to cushion tumbling and running and smooth pavement that's perfect for riding toys and drawing in chalk. Set up a child-sized picnic table for snacks and crafts.

Allow plenty of clearance around climbing structures and swings, with soft mulch or rubber padding underfoot for gentle landings. Include storage for riding toys, assorted balls, pogo sticks, jump ropes, and perhaps some water toys for the warmer months.

Double the fun
Not many children can resist the messy pleasures of a classic sandbox, *far right*. When sand play ends, it can be covered with a large-scale game board, *right*, for another level of fun and games.

Planning for portability

Children are always eager to play and explore, both inside and out

A child's zest for play extends far beyond the playroom, however extensively equipped it may be. She'll undoubtedly want to explore outdoors, too, and will likely want to take some of the "great indoors" along with her. Buckets and baskets are useful for transporting diversions such as paper and colored pencils to the yard for some alfresco sketching.

And sturdy tote bags and backpacks are a must for carrying toys, books, snacks, and the other supplies your child may need when going farther afield, say, to a play date. Lightweight folding tables may come in handy for holding supplies. A portable shelter, such as a blanket over a card table, or even a tent or tepee, keep children cozy wherever they roam.

Movable havens
With portable environments like this canvas tepee, *left and far left*, children can create their own space-within-a-space.

Encouraging active play

With their mesmerizing powers of entertainment and enticing glow, computers, TVs, and video games can lure kids away from active play. Virtual reality is fine in small doses, but children also relish contact with the real world and the people who inhabit it. Channeling family time into interactive outdoor pursuits, such as swimming and biking, isn't just fun: it fosters a lifelong love of activity.

Media savvy

Since modern media offer enriching, exciting possibilities for kids, most parents aim not for a total ban, but for a balance with a healthy range of other activities. Some families keep TVs and computers in common areas so adults can monitor more easily the content and the time spent using them. Setting a timer during children's computer sessions can impartially remind them when it's time to move on to some other pursuits. And when parents and other adults review and discuss TV programs, movies, and websites with their children, kids learn to think about media more critically.

Simple pleasures

Today's children often get excited about low-tech games such as "Simon Says," "Red Light, Green Light," or "Kick the Can" – old favorites that are new to them. If you're unfamiliar with the rules, refer to the many books and websites (search for "childhood games" online) that help preserve the rich lore of youth. One of the facts you might pick up, for instance, is that children from South America to Asia play hopping games with squares drawn on the ground.

Your family can join in that tradition by creating a classic hopscotch game on a driveway, sidewalk, or basement floor. You can make a temporary hopscotch area with colored chalk or masking tape, or a permanent one with paint. Once you've laid out the single and side-by-side squares numbered from 1 to 10, explain the rules. In one version, a player tosses a small stone into successive squares, then hops a round trip through the squares, standing on one foot in the single squares, and with one foot in each of the paired squares. On her way back, she pauses to pick up the stone. Missing a square, putting a foot down, or stepping on lines means the forfeit of a turn.

eating

Fostering healthy habits

During a family meal, children learn about good nutrition and the pleasure of sharing food, time, and stories. With today's busy schedules and enticing ads for less-healthy foods (many parents wish that spinach had an equivalent ad campaign), orchestrating nutritious family meals takes a bit of effort. But these oases in our daily lives can be preserved through canny scheduling – and by designing dining areas that are both attractive and convenient.

Time and patience are key to fostering a good diet. When children are exposed to new foods amid familiar favorites, and given role models of wholesome eating, their tastes will gradually grow more adventurous.

Stocking the pantry with nutritious food allows parents to relax a bit and let their child choose from the healthy choices readily available to them. Despite the idiosyncrasies of kids' tastes, a child's favorites, chosen from a range of healthful foods, will likely add up to a reasonably balanced diet over time – even if it entails some leftover dinner vegetables at breakfast!

THE WAITING GAME
A personalized pocket hung
on the back of a chair holds
a diversion to occupy a hungry
toddler. (**See page 92** for details.)

PRACTICALITY UNDERFOOT
The blond wood floor used in both
kitchen and dining room is coated
with a polyurethane finish to help
it withstand spilled food, dropped
cups, and other eating mishaps.

A CHEERFUL MEDLEY
Mix-and-match dinnerware in colorful hues brightens a casual table. And because it's made of sturdy plastic, the set won't be ruined by broken pieces.

PERSONAL TOUCHES
To craft a unique and practical place mat, laminate your child's drawings or cover them with clear peel-and-stick plastic. (**See page 98** for details.)

HEALTHY SNACKS
Keep kids' hunger at bay between meals with plastic containers of bite-sized, nutritious snacks such as carrot sticks or fruit.

ROOM TO MOVE
A round table with a pedestal base opens up the leg room, so it's easy to pull a child's chair alongside your own or squeeze in a guest.

ADAPTABLE SEATING
To welcome a small child to the grown-up table, add a booster seat and keep the table settings low so he can see across easily.

Rethinking the kitchen

The heart of the house is a place for activity, nourishment, and family fun

Since young children are still learning about sitting still and eating neatly, it makes sense to design a dining area where you all can feel at ease. Floors of vinyl, laminates, tile, or polyurethaned wood, and tabletops of laminates or painted wood, can be maintained with a quick swipe. Once the stage of tablecloth tugging passes, you can bring back some easy-care table linens.

Even if your little one doesn't sit in one place for long, establish the routine of coming to the table for meals. Give your child plenty of notice before dinner, then let her help you put the last few things on the table – or set her up with a toy or drawing pad so she can be happily occupied until dinner is served.

Sophie

Kid-proof your tabletop
Colorful, dishwasher-safe plastic plates, stain-resistant table surfaces, and a wipe-clean bib, *above*, all come in handy when young diners first move from a high chair to a seat at the family table.

A handy diversion
This washable hanging toy bag, *left*, welcomes a little girl to her chair. The bag is made from a prehemmed linen tea towel attached with grommets and cords from a sewing store, and its pocket is a stitched-on washcloth simply personalized with bright fabric paint.

An inviting picture
Creamy cotton doorway drapes, *right*, frame a family-style kitchen. When closed, they create a graceful backdrop for the more formal dining room while concealing the "backstage" preparation area.

" Squirty oranges are one of my favorite snacks **"**

Personalizing the table

Your child's artwork can brighten the tabletop with spirited colors and patterns

Every chef appreciates the value of clever presentation. While daily table settings can be kept simple, children are easy to impress with details such as a fancy serving bowl, special birthday plates, a cheerful pitcher filled with flowers, or even some mesmerizing candles (kept safely out of reach). To put their stamp on the mealtime experience, most children will enthusiastically contribute their handmade artwork. They can make personalized plates, cups, and bowls by using craft kits at home or visiting a ceramic shop specializing in kids' crafts. Or you can buy plastic cups and mugs that allow you to insert your child's photo, a favorite artwork, or even a snapshot of a treasured pet.

Children can create their own unique tableware with a craft kit.

1 Buy a plate-decorating kit, which can be found in many craft or toy stores, or by searching online for "plate-making kit."

2 Give your child the kit's circular template and some felt-tipped pens, and let him unleash his imagination.

3 Mail your child's artwork in the supplied envelope, and receive dishwasher-safe tableware.

A sense of identity
Kids love to make their mark by writing their names and expressing themselves through art, *left*, so personalized plates, *far left*, are always favorites.

Making mealtimes enjoyable

Plan ahead for more relaxed meals. You'll cut down on last-minute decisions by deciding on a week's worth of dinners at once, which gives you more time each evening to enlist your kids in food preparation. Helping you in the kitchen hones useful skills and may foster enthusiasm for the meal to come. Involve kids in the table talk, too, asking questions to prompt stories about their day.

Setting an example

Introducing children to the basics of table manners and etiquette starts as soon as they're able to join the family at the kitchen or dining-room table. Observing how others interact while eating helps kids eventually understand the mealtime routine. The key is to make it enjoyable for children to participate.

Learning to set a table is one of the first steps kids can take to help. Even toddlers will enjoy putting the napkins, utensils, and other unbreakables on the table. They're likely to be even more pleased to contribute an artistic touch by making custom place mats.

One idea is to create an educational "blueprint" of a perfect place setting by gluing construction-paper cutouts on a backing of colorful poster board. These cutouts should show exactly where the plate, cup, napkin, and utensils go.

To make this or one of your child's artworks into a durable, wipeable place mat, have it laminated at an office-supply store, or simply cover it with clear peel-and-stick plastic. Either way, she can proudly display her artwork on the table at every meal, and it just might make her more excited about the true task at hand – eating a healthy meal!

learning

Stimulating children's minds

With their curiosity and willingness to experiment, children learn through all they explore, touch, build, and ponder. And despite the current push toward early academics, kids are masters at learning the old-fashioned way: through experience, observation, and creative play.

Learning proceeds at its own pace – sometimes in methodical steps, sometimes in creative leaps. By engaging in wide-ranging conversations, building on your child's strengths, and providing the raw materials for exploration, you help your child not just learn, but delight in the process.

Tailor your child's surroundings to his or her learning style. The hands-on artist or scientist will need space for messy artworks or experiments, while a contemplative visual learner might love colorful posters and a quiet window seat for reading. The musical child may want a practice area and storage for instruments, and the young athlete will delight in an exercise mat, a chin-up bar, and a bookshelf full of inspiring sports stories.

ILLUMINATING IDEAS
In a multipurpose corner ready for work, study, and play, shades of transparent bamboo temper the warm natural light.

CENTRAL COMPUTING
Placing the computer in a shared family workspace makes it easier to help kids with technical glitches and supervise their web surfing.

A PERSONAL TOUCH
Show your child he's made his mark by putting his photo, artwork, and some cherished keepsakes on view.

A MODULAR MIX
File cabinets topped with long counters provide flexible workspace and storage that can be adjusted to suit your family's changing needs and interests.

READY REFERENCES
Keeping maps, reference books, and charts easily accessible prompts kids to tap into available resources.

VISUAL INSPIRATIONS
Having crafts, photos, and art supplies on view cheers up the space and encourages new leaps of inspiration.

ROOM TO SPREAD OUT
Setting up work surfaces in a horseshoe shape makes the most of office space designed to accommodate the entire family.

BE SEATED
Height-adjustable rolling chairs can seat almost everyone in the family. This chair's base swivels 360 degrees, making it easier for an adult to turn around and check on the kids.

Working together

A family office serves separate pursuits while fostering a sense of togetherness

Families love sitting down to work on projects together – especially if the seats are comfortable, the workspace is appealing, and the appropriate materials are close at hand. With the right design, a shared work area can meet an entire family's needs. In this room, an adult desk, storage cubbies, bookcases, and versatile desktops set on file cabinets (modular units that can be reconfigured easily as needs change) team up with a child-sized table and a handpainted chalkboard (see pages 59 and 110 for more details). Targeted lighting enhances the natural light, while cheerful desk accessories, graphic wall art, and colorful toys and art supplies add whimsical touches to the industrious atmosphere.

Space that computes
It's easier to encourage savvy and responsible computer use when the machine is set up in a family area, *above*. As children's computing time becomes longer, the ergonomics of the work area should be tailored to young users.

A wealth of choices
In this corner of the family office, *left*, a child might draw on a mini-chalkboard, write a letter or school composition at the desk, or curl up on the sofa to read.

Colorful accents
The child-sized table and chairs, *right*, are perfect for games, art projects, and other youthful pursuits. The spacious shelf unit conveniently holds books, educational toys, and oversize letters and numerals that reinforce developing skills while adding charm to the room.

"Let's go where they don't have to eat broccoli "

Learning by doing

Hands-on experimentation shows children there are many different ways to create

Spaces for learning need to combine desks, chairs, tables, and storage, plus a few props to encourage open-ended creation and play. The essential ingredients might include books, building sets, dress-up gear, musical instruments, science experiments, art supplies, and educational games. The elements needn't be elaborate; in fact, kids often discover that the simplest materials, like crayons or clay, are the most versatile. Supply your child's favorites – and add new ones to the mix now and again to keep things interesting.

Fine motor skills for table work develop in the preschool years. While kids are honing their skills, make things easier for them with esay-to-grasp crayons and chalk.

Easy writer
A chalkboard tabletop, *right and far right,* provides an enticing space for a child to practice sums, write out the alphabet, or perhaps create an artistic masterpiece.

Expanding horizons

Open your child's eyes with a bedroom that colorfully evokes faraway places

For a stimulating wall display, it's hard to beat maps. They introduce the notion of distant countries, instill a sense of wonder at our vast and varied world, and encourage representational thinking. If you mount inexpensive local or international maps on foam backing, your child can mark meaningful sites with pushpins. A laminated wall-wide map, *right and below*, lets children outline both real and imaginary journeys with dry-erase pens. If your child's a budding geographer or explorer, postcards collected from friends, art from school reports, souvenirs from faraway cities, and vivid nautical flags will enhance the globe-trotting feeling of the room.

Showcasing interests

Lively displays of mementos and found objects celebrate your child's world

Learning spaces can showcase a child's enthusiasms, whether for swimming, animals, dance, space exploration, or sports. Playing up your child's current interests says that they're worth exploring further. And working with children to create themed displays teaches them how one idea can unite disparate objects. For instance, a horse lover might juxtapose horse pictures, a show ribbon, and a horseshoe. To record a vacation, a map of the route could form the backdrop for souvenirs, photos, and a plane ticket. A shelf or shadow box unifies assorted objects and keeps thematic displays down to a manageable size, since a room dominated by one interest might too easily be outgrown.

3-D displays

Create a display of objects and pictures in an array of rustic, simply constructed shadow boxes.

1 Purchase pine boards of the desired dimensions, and cut to appropriate lengths for the height and width of the finished frame.

2 Join the pieces at the corners, gluing and then hammering the sides into the crosspieces' cut ends with small finishing nails.

3 Paint or stain the frames and let dry before mounting on the wall.

4 Join your child in filling the shadow box with pictures and lightweight mementos grouped around a common theme.

Souvenirs of the shore
Shadow boxes can frame themed displays, such as shells and photos evoking a family beach vacation, *far left*. Maps and exotic keepsakes, *left*, might inspire a budding geographer, who in this room used the letter "E" to mark the east wall.

Keeping books handy

Scattering good reading material around your home encourages children to pick up a book whenever the mood strikes them

Children begin independent reading on their own timetable. But parents can foster this skill by reading to children and showing their own pleasure in the written word. With so many diversions competing for your child's attention, give the joys of reading equal time by keeping books and magazines handy in baskets, bookcases, and on tables beside comfortable, well-lit chairs. Even after your child starts reading on his or her own, continue to enjoy books together as well, so that you can answer questions and teach the fine art of reading between the lines.

Casual but collected
Bookcases are space efficient, but adding some less-formal storage, *left*, incorporates reading materials into the flow of activity, ensuring that books and magazines are always in view and easily accessible.

Playful displays
A sturdy vintage wagon, *right*, maintains its jaunty attitude even while taking on a new role of storing and displaying books. This movable feast of reading material easily relocates to a favorite reading spot.

Encouraging exploration

Nobody tells a baby "Now it's time to start rolling over" or "Now it's time to talk." We just look on, impressed and amazed, as our child makes these leaps in development. As they grow, children continue to follow their personal timetables for acquiring skills and knowledge. Foster that drive to learn by introducing kids to new experiences and encouraging experimentation within safe guidelines.

Provide the raw materials

Offer your child some inspiring ingredients for creative work and play, then step back and admire what he or she cooks up. As skills and goals expand, your child will discover a broader range of possibilities with the same versatile basics like markers, paper, crayons, and clay. For many kids, computers have become another essential tool.

Store materials for learning in easy-to-understand categories, and in low cubbies, baskets, translucent plastic drawers, and cupboards. With the tools at the ready, your child won't have to ask permission to begin exploring a new idea.

Lessons from nature

Children love the wide-open, tactile, ever-changing world of nature, whether they're stomping around in the woods, on sandy beaches, or in their own neighborhood park or backyard. Besides being fun, outdoor explorations provide valuable exercise and enriching exposure to the textures, sounds, smells, and other mysteries of the physical world. And nature teaches children lasting lessons about change, continuity, beauty, and the interdependence of all living things.

Many kids are born collectors. If you provide just a shelf or two, children can create their own personal museum of natural history to show off the sticks, rocks, leaves, or shells found on nature walks. (It also might help keep the items from accidentally going through a wash cycle crammed in a pocket.) Use clear plastic jars or open bowls to store and display small articles. Display flat items, like leaves, in clear plastic sleeves. Keep some field guides handy so you can help your child identify his most exciting finds. Some kids will want to label the objects in their collection, adding details such as the place where they found their specimens and the date of discovery.

bathing

Creating a family-friendly bath

Lives change, families grow, and bathrooms have to accommodate your new requirements. You've probably adapted this essential room in several ways for your children, or you may even have a "kids' bathroom" tailored specifically for them. And youngsters do put their fair share of demands on the space, with less-than-neat toothbrushing and long, delightfully splashy baths.

When it comes to storage, there are two key goals for a family bathroom: keep necessities within children's reach, and store medications, shaving supplies, and cleaning products safely out of range. Other precautions include fitting electrical outlets with protective devices, installing an easy-release door lock, and moderating water temperature.

Many parents prefer to keep the tile and fixtures simple, layering on kid-pleasing colors and patterns. Graphic wallpaper borders, decoratively painted walls, sinkside accessories, and bright, fluffy towels and scatter rugs all add visual appeal. And don't forget the tub-toy collection.

WINDOW DRESSING
Translucent, wipeable roll-up shades provide privacy while maximizing the warm sunniness of a wide-windowed bathroom.

OVER-THE-TUB SHELF
A plastic, wire, or wooden shelf that sits atop the tub keeps soaps, bubble bath, and maybe even a family of rubber ducks within a bather's reach.

HANGING SOLUTIONS
A coated-wire basket suspended over the bathtub is a great way to keep toys handy for tub time – and to allow them to drip-dry afterward.

ADDED STORAGE
Tubside baskets, lined with decorative scalloped hand towels, hold washcloths and toys until the next bathtime. (**See page 131** for details.)

SOFTNESS UNDERFOOT
Although easy to maintain, tile floors can be a chilly surprise after a warm bath. A nonslip cotton rug eases the transition.

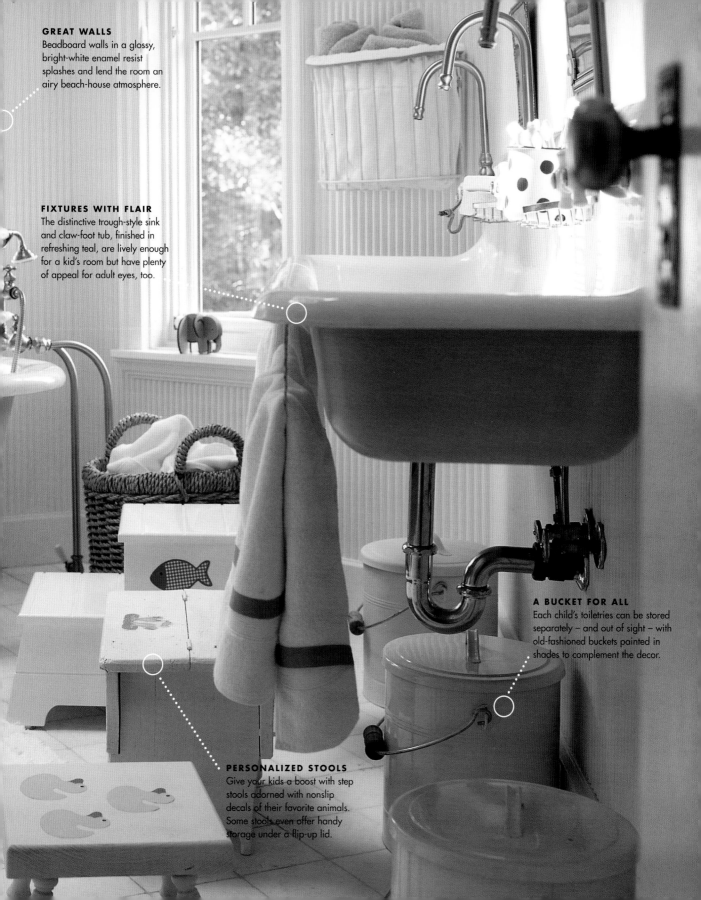

GREAT WALLS
Beadboard walls in a glossy, bright-white enamel resist splashes and lend the room an airy beach-house atmosphere.

FIXTURES WITH FLAIR
The distinctive trough-style sink and claw-foot tub, finished in refreshing teal, are lively enough for a kid's room but have plenty of appeal for adult eyes, too.

A BUCKET FOR ALL
Each child's toiletries can be stored separately – and out of sight – with old-fashioned buckets painted in shades to complement the decor.

PERSONALIZED STOOLS
Give your kids a boost with step stools adorned with nonslip decals of their favorite animals. Some stools even offer handy storage under a flip-up lid.

Tailoring the room to kids

For inspiration, approach the details from a kid's-eye perspective

With a few smart adaptations, children can feel at home in any bathroom. For better access, it's a good idea to keep a sturdy, nonskid step stool near the sink, and to install faucet handles suited to little hands. Mount a mirror on the wall at your child's eye level, and a towel rack and clothing hooks at a reachable height. You can encourage independence by keeping everyday necessities such as hairbrushes, accessories, toothbrushes, toothpaste, and bathing needs in a vanity's low drawer or in a basket kept on a low shelf or even the floor. Baskets, tins, and handpainted racks and shelves can perform double duty as both space-efficient storage and decorative flourishes that brighten the bathroom.

Premium sink space
Zero in on the daily essentials used at the sink, then organize them attractively in colorful containers, such as this big polka-dot enamelware cup, *above*.

Water works
With easy-to-turn faucet handles and mirrors mounted at kid height, *left*, this sink makes it easier for children to get ready for the day on their own.

Streamlining rush hour
The trough-style family sink, *right*, makes it easy to share space. Each child's daily toiletries are stowed in a painted bucket underneath. At the bottom of the sink, fabric loops hold towels color-coordinated with the mirrors. Nonslip tub decals further personalize each child's area.

" You look funny with bubbles on your head "

Storing tub-time gear

To make a place for everything, use imaginative storage containers

When assessing the storage that will best suit your family bathroom, focus on function. Often-used items are best kept on view, while infrequently used ones can be neatly tucked away. Bathing areas benefit from holders for washcloths, soap, and shampoo. Over-the-tub baskets or mesh bags allow ventilation so waterlogged toys can drain easily. The sink area

is prone to overflow with soaps, brushes, cups, and toothbrushes. Adding shelves, hooks, and towel bars makes the most of wall space. Baskets and bins add color while separating each user's lineup of toiletries. Consider borrowing storage ideas from other rooms, too, such as spice racks, canisters, and unbreakable enamelware.

Making tubside caddies

Open-air storage keeps tub toys dry, fresh, and always at hand for the next bathing beauty.

1 For tubside storage, choose coated wire baskets, *left,* that mount with magnets or suction cups.

2 Buy two terry cloth hand towels with decorative scalloped edges to create matching basket liners that are absorbent and washable.

3 Sew the two towels together lengthwise, then sew up the sides.

4 Place the towels in the baskets, fold over the towel edges, and finish them with a bow or ribbon trim.

5 Stock the basket with your child's favorite lightweight bath toys, washcloths, and sponges.

Bathing buddies
Use your bathroom's available space for storage add-ons, such as these decorative tub-mounted caddies, *left,* to keep bathing necessities dry and within easy reach.

Making washing up more fun

Most kids are drawn to water in all forms – oceans, lakes, puddles, rain – and will linger happily in the bathtub. A regularly scheduled bath helps children shift gears from other activities, especially if bathtime is leisurely enough to allow for lots of play. Since kids need supervision around water, add a chair to the bath area. You'll be more comfortable as you help with the sudsing and rinsing.

Personalize bathroom gear

Children will more easily pick out their own toiletries if you let them choose a favorite color and use it to color-code their daily essentials. By purchasing a few inexpensive products and dressing up some others with appliqués, decals, or paint, you can create individual ensembles of the staples – towel, step stool, toothbrush, hairbrush, and cup – in a favorite hue, such as fire-engine red or vivid aqua. As a side benefit, this color-coded system means there won't have to be any more discussions about who left a towel on the bathroom floor!

Awash in fun

Bathtime becomes playtime – and learning time – with water toys that float, pour, stack, squirt, and nest. Include some large plastic bowls, funnels, straws, measuring cups, and colanders from the kitchen. Don't even hint that such explorations are hands-on lessons in measuring, adding, and subtracting. Encourage more experimentation and creative play by offering water-ready art supplies, such as special bath crayons and paints, and tub stick-ons in assorted shapes and letters. Toddlers enjoy paging through waterproof plastic picture books in the tub, while older kids might appreciate an over-the-tub book rest or even a simple board to hold a magazine or a paperback.

Don't forget the possibilities of the shower. On a practical level, a handheld tub fixture can provide a final rinse cycle after a bubble bath. And kids will be intrigued by a feature seen in warm-climate homes: an outside shower. But they can also have fun with a simpler outdoor shower kit attached to a hose outlet, which lets them get a quick rinse to wash off sand or dirt, or the chlorine from a pool.

sleeping

Getting ready for bed

At day's end, a child's focus shifts away from the waking world's enticing distractions to the quieter pleasures of relaxation, stories, and sleep. A well-ordered bedroom filled with familiar things and favorite colors eases the transition from full-on activity to tranquil slumber.

Your child's bed – be it a classic four-poster, a country-style trundle, or a space-saving bunk – is the focal point that sets the decorative tone of the room. Bedding is important, too. Ask your child to help you pick out sheets and a comforter, which could be coordinated in motifs such as bold plaids, pastel flowers, or bright geometric patterns.

Targeted storage like a peg for a robe, a basket for slippers, and a bookshelf for nightly stories makes the bedtime routine smoother. Other thoughtful touches include a soft chenille rug beside the bed, a reading light, and a nightstand holding water and a kid-sized flashlight within arm's reach. Your child will feel nestled in a haven that's perfect for winding down from a busy day, dreaming of wonderful places and fanciful characters, and resting up for tomorrow's adventures.

SHEER CANOPY
A gossamer canopy of white fabric lends a little girl's bed some storybook charm.

BOOK NOOK
A bedside rack that displays books face out makes it easy for kids to recognize and pick a story to ease them into slumber.

LAYERS OF COMFORT
Waffle- and jacquard-weave blankets, a matelassé spread, and cotton percale sheets create layers that you can adjust easily to ensure that your child is comfortable and warm.

BOUNTIFUL BASKETS
Pajamas, socks, and slippers are easily accessible in a series of matching woven baskets hung from the bed's footboard. (**See page 146** for details.)

WINDOW DRESSING
Linen Roman shades tied with bows echo the bed's gauzy canopy and add an air of elegance to the bedroom.

READERS' CHAIRS
Appropriately sized chairs, placed next to a display of children's books, encourage impromptu reading at any time of the day.

PICTURE GALLERY
Kids feel like they're in "their" space with favorite artworks hung with decorative ribbons on the bedroom walls.

LIFE STORIES
Criss-crossed ribbons tacked on a wooden toy chest create a bulletin board ideal for displaying photos of family, friends, and pets.

WALL-TO-WALL CARPET
A durable wool carpet (or a colorful chenille rug) gives a child's bedroom a cozy look while keeping bare feet cushioned and warm as they step out into a new day.

Reading for relaxation

Bedtime books lull drowsy children with flowing words and turning pages

A love of reading develops early on, usually on someone's lap. Planning your child's room to make nighttime reading comfortable gives this fundamental skill some warm, pleasant associations. With a full-sized armchair, or large cushions propped against a bed's headboard, parent and child can settle down together. Engage a small child in a story by using dramatic voices and sound effects, pausing often to ask, "What do you think happened next?" Run your finger along the words to show how the text flows and to point out recurring phrases or names – or to let your child "read" the story's familiar or rhyming words. As kids become independent readers, they'll still love story time.

Ready for reading
A kid-sized chair, *above*, offers a place to settle in with a story and provides convenient and casual book storage.

Create a colorful mini-library
Your child can quickly spot her favorite stories with a bookshelf that's made to display book covers face-out, *left*. And as your child's attention span grows, she'll appreciate having her current book waiting on the nightstand – ready for more adventures to unfold that evening.

Snuggling in with a story
Once a child is old enough to enjoy books independently, she's bound to relish reading in bed, especially if she's resting against a luxuriously plump pillow with a beloved doll at her side, *right*.

" I only like stories with happy endings **"**

Making a bed cozy

Soft fabrics and easy-to-reach essentials make for a comfortable bedroom

When choosing the best bedding, consider one of a child's most acute senses: touch. Children delight in a duvet's light, fluffy warmth, and cotton sheets with a high thread count stay soft and smooth through frequent washings. Other favorite fabrics include velvet, flannel, chenille, and even faux fur. Once you've set up your child's soft nest, surround it with useful storage. It could be built into the bed itself, like a trundle bed's roomy drawers or a headboard with niches and shelves. A bed skirt can conceal under-bed baskets, rollaway bins, and boxes. Or improvise some of your own whimsical bedside storage, such as the fabric pouches shown here or the baskets on the next page.

Sewing bedside pockets

Hanging storage pouches can organize bedtime supplies, such as books and a flashlight.

1 Buy a yard (about 1 meter) of 45"-wide (114cm) white canvas. Prewash the fabric, iron it, and then cut out three 8 x 9" (20 x 23cm) rectangles for the pockets.

2 Hem and miter the three pockets and a 24 x 33" (61 x 84cm) piece to make the main canvas panel. Use 5/8" (1.6cm) hems and seams.

3 Sew a decorative ribbon on the top edge of each pocket.

4 Evenly space the pockets on the large panel, pin them in place, then sew them on using a topstitch.

5 Slip the panel's other end, about 18" (46cm) of fabric, under the mattress so it stays securely in place.

Pocket organizers
Small items, easily lost among covers and pillows, are kept in bedside pouches that harmonize with the bed's soft look, *far left*.

Adding bedside storage

Your child will feel safe and snug in bed if she's surrounded by her favorite things

Baskets are a simple way to add storage to the bed area.

1 Purchase some small, lightweight wicker or plastic baskets to hang along the width of the footboard.

2 Thread color-coordinated ribbon or cord through the rim of each container, leaving enough room to secure the cord to the footboard.

3 If you can, simply tie each basket to the bedframe. Otherwise, mark spots on the footboard (below the mattress level), where you'd like to secure the ribbons. Drill shallow holes in each spot, taking care not to pierce through the wood to the outside of the footboard. Insert a vinyl-coated screw eye (sold in hardware stores) into each hole. Tie the cord or ribbon to each hook.

4 Adjust the length of the cords or ribbons so that the baskets dangle gracefully from the footboard.

When creating bedroom storage, think about what your child would most like to have within arm's reach. It might be a robe or pajamas kept handy on a peg or rack, or books and plush toys arranged on accessible shelves. If the bed is topped with decorative pillows, toys, and extra blankets, place a bench or bin nearby so they can be stored out of the way when it's time for sleep. Another option is to loop baskets over the bed's footboard to hold bedtime staples (or sew some bedside pockets, as shown on the previous pages). Give a place of honor to comfort objects, like much-loved blankets. Since the baskets' contents are visible, it will be easy for your child to find just what she's looking for.

Bedside buddies
Open baskets hanging from the foot of the bed, *far right*, provide visual cues that help children find pajamas, flashlights, or even company for the night ahead, *right.*

Sharing bedroom space

With the right setup, siblings can stay true to themselves while still finding plenty of common ground

In a shared bedroom, children learn valuable lessons in cooperation and compromise. But at the same time they can still make their mark on the room, displaying their individual style with color choices, bedding preferences, and other flourishes of personalized decoration.

Bunk beds, with secure railings and anchored ladders, make the most of a small shared space for children age six and older. And trundle beds help with limited (and shared) storage space by stowing each child's gear out of sight in an under-bed drawer.

In perfect agreement
Matching beds and linens provide symmetry and a tidy look to a shared room, *left*, while reversible comforters and assorted pillows still offer plenty of mix-and-match potential.

A rainbow of possibilities
Sleeping spaces with built-in bunks (pictured here without the guardrails), *right*, can be both compact and stylish. Children can choose a color scheme for their individual bed nook, and the room will retain a harmonious look if the bedding patterns match.

Setting a bedtime routine

Most kids (and adults, too) need nightly routines to ease them toward sleep. Each child is different, so experiment with ways to signal that transition. You might start with a timer that chimes to remind your child to wrap up the day's activities. Then putting on pajamas, brushing teeth, and reading an agreed-upon number of storybooks could lead into soothing back rubs and lullabies.

Sound decisions

Quiet surroundings can encourage peaceful sleeping (though some kids find a little bit of household noise reassuring). For better sound control, place your child's bed near the quietest wall in her room and add sound-absorbing rugs and drapes, and perhaps some lulling "white noise" from a fan or air filter. After story time is over, some children like to drift off to sleep while they listen to soft music or a recorded story. Include a CD player and a selection of favorites by your child's bed to ease the journey into slumber.

Assemble a dream kit

The reassuring presence of a few toys and accessories that appear night after night can signal to your child that it's time to rest. To keep those items' sleep-inducing magic on tap, you and your child can create a "dream kit" to hold them.

Simply gather some of her favorite soothing things and keep them in a basket or quilted bag that's always stored by the bed. Ask your child to help you pick out her sleep-time essentials. Dream-kit contents might include favored pajamas, a few treasured storybooks, a well-loved fuzzy blanket, and a doll or plush toy. She may want to put her name on the bag or basket that will house her dream kit, or decorate it with ribbons or colorful pins.

Being able to assemble and adjust the kit's contents might make your child feel more in control of the process of taking an afternoon nap and going to bed each night. The dream kit also can serve as a handy take-along for sleepovers and travel, something that will help your child feel at home even when she's in unfamiliar surroundings.

organizing

Keeping the family organized

Children and their gear have a wonderful way of turning a household into a home. Toys on the coffee table, puppets and a stage in a family room, and sports equipment in the entryway bring a sense of activity even when the kids are asleep. Thoughtful organization can keep all these things in order, freeing up time for life's more fulfilling pursuits.

Much of family life is spontaneous, but targeted storage can simplify the daily rituals of dinnertime, playtime, bathtime, and bedtime. When organizing any room, the basic principles are generally sound guidelines: shed excess, categorize and group what's left, and designate containers to hold it all. Balance open storage, with its visual cues and easy access, with closed storage, which gives a room a finished look.

Store things where they're first used – or where they tend to end up. For instance, add a living-room shelf for supplies if your child creates art at the coffee table, or a basket for all the shoes that wind up in the front hall. Make it almost as easy to put an object in its well-defined home as it is to just drop it somewhere random "for now."

JOB POSTINGS
Help kids remember their chores with individual chalkboards that remind them of their duties – and give them the satisfaction of erasing the tasks they've completed.

MESSAGE CENTER
Personalized corkboards give children a place to look for party invitations, mail, and sports schedules. (**See page 158** for details.)

CREATIVE CONTAINERS
By placing a variety of open and closed baskets and bins on the floor, you keep storage where kids can see and use it.

DOUBLE DUTY
A cabinet that doubles as a bench comes in handy in an entryway. Not only does it add storage, kids can sit on it to put on and take off their shoes.

ANN
• SET TABLE
• PULL WEEDS
• READ

MILES
• CLEAR TABLE
• WATER PLANTS
• READ

COLE
• SWEEP
• GET MAIL
• READ

MESSAGES
TIM called can you come over to play

HOOKED ON STORAGE
Surround your entryways with child-height pegs and racks for backpacks, purses, and other heading-out-the-door essentials.

SONALIZED CUBBIES
e plates and fun pictorial s show children where to their coats, shoes, scarves, other belongings. (**See** e 165 for additional ideas ersonalizing storage.)

30

FLOORING DECISIONS
Mudrooms often live up to their name. Well-placed doormats, washable rugs, and durable, water-resistant floors are good ways to keep dirt at bay.

A SOLUTION FOR SHOES
Keeping a basket or rack for footwear near the door is a convenient way to store shoes and minimize muddy footprints.

Making an entrance

Smart entryway storage gets kids out the door – and stores what they bring back

The entryway is the crossroads of your house. It's a place of exits and entrances, which, when it comes to children, often means a fair amount of things to keep track of and store. The list varies with each family, but it usually includes kids' shoes, coats, outdoor toys, school supplies, and gear for a host of activities. One way to keep it all organized is the time-tested mudroom, a transitional room with durable materials and targeted storage. Even if your home doesn't have a separate entrance room, your entryway can ease comings and goings with a bench for tying shoes, a rack where coats can drip-dry, and bulletin boards to display invitations, school announcements, and other notices.

Artful reminders

Raise the signal flag on an antique mailbox, *above*, to remind little ones to look inside for homework or school forms to take along that morning. Even if it's as simple as an "out" basket, a spot for daily papers helps keep children organized when they head out the door.

Paper chase

Bulletin boards can keep flyers, party invitations, and sports schedules front and center, *left*. Here, each child's individual board reflects his or her interests and activities, plus a few favorite pictures, postcards, and keepsakes.

Transition point

This well-planned mudroom, *right*, combines a washable rug, ventilated storage for wet shoes, pegs for backpacks, accessible low storage, and an array of sporting equipment mounted on the wall.

"Why does this ball always run away from me"

Putting things in place

Special equipment, like an array of sports gear, is kept ready for action

Keep sports equipment organized and handy with perforated hardboard panels and hooks.

1 If the standard 4 x 8′ (1.2 x 2.4 meters) tempered pegboard doesn't fit your space, cut it to fit – or ask the retailer to do it for you.

2 Mount a framing board so it underlies the panel's top edge, anchoring it to wall studs with wood screws in predrilled holes. Add a few vertical supports, too.

3 Attach the pegboard to the framing boards with construction adhesive and wood screws.

4 Add a mix of hooks and anchors for a space-efficient arrangement of your child's sporting gear.

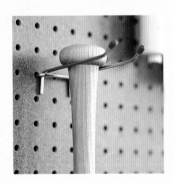

On the level
A pegboard, *right*, holds much-used items within a child's reach. And by standing on a storage bench, kids can reach items stored higher up on the wall, *far right*.

As children develop new interests, storage should evolve along with them. The mudroom that once held toddler shoes and soap-bubble wands may later house sports equipment and backpacks. Take an inventory of your child's gear regularly, so you can apply the best storage solutions. Are you dealing with large, awkward items, such as a baseball backstop, or just a bevy of smaller objects? Which items in daily use need easy-to-reach storage? Group related objects, and then store them where a child can find them. Storage benches and large baskets are useful for bulky items; drawers and cubbies are ideal for smaller ones. Pegboards, long used in workshops for wall-mounting tools, can do the same for sports gear.

Personalizing storage

Label storage spaces to help wandering objects find their way back home

Not all kids are into neatness for its own sake, but most will notice that keeping track of their stuff saves time for more important pursuits, like playing soccer or getting in some practice time for the next music lesson. If you allocated storage to different family members – and perhaps even to their various activities – your child will know where to find things (and maybe even where to put them back).

By labeling storage containers with words or pictures, you provide useful visual reminders. Containers should be manageable for small hands, with contents on view. If a child can grab something easily without taking other things out, the whole area stays tidier.

Portable organizers
Imaginatively crafted labels, *far left*, spell out what's inside each wooden caddy. And kids on the go can easily carry such small, shallow containers, *left*.

Setting up good communications

By keeping tabs on schoolwork, chores, and social schedules, you're teaching your child about organizing time

It's wonderful that your child has a wide circle of friends and a growing range of interests, but the packed schedule that results requires a system to keep track of each day's events. In many households, the solution is a master calendar that everyone can refer to. Calendars, bulletin boards, and message centers also provide kids with reminders about what they might want to wear or take along that day – as well as giving them a reassuring sense that everyone in the family is accounted for back at home base.

Scheduling the fun stuff

In addition to the family's master schedule, a children's calendar crafted from a basic pegboard and colorful yarn, *left*, shows a child's play dates, parties, and athletic events. Notes and invitations are simply attached with miniature clothespins.

Communication central

If you set up a chalkboard message center, *right*, your child will always know where to look for, or leave, day-to-day notes and reminders – whether they involve vital information or fun, affectionate greetings.

Bringing order to the wardrobe

An expansive storage space for clothes and shoes rises to its full potential when it's divided into savvy sections

A wide-open closet with a single clothes rod looks wonderfully roomy, and its capacity multiplies when you partition the space into a variety of storage sections. The upper shelves can be reserved for rarely used items, while lower levels and benches keep everyday clothing and shoes handy. Hanging storage is less crucial for children's casual clothes than drawers and shelves to hold underwear, T-shirts, and jeans. And children love the easy access offered by bins, racks, and pegs.

Closet creations
A wall with built-in drawers, *left*, is the basis of a new "closet" with the addition of a clothing rod and elegant drapes. The dresser is framed by storage benches, where a child can sit to put on shoes or climb up to reach hanging clothes.

Small details
In this bedroom storage area, the casually labeled hatboxes and fuchsia tote bag, *right*, are a decorative way to organize and store a child's small accessories.

Improvising storage spaces

Kids learning to organize their belongings might be surprised to hear that even grown-ups sometimes need help gathering their things. Having smart storage spaces can make organization almost instinctual. Finding a place for everything takes ingenuity, though. Look high for places to install shelves and racks, and low for nooks to tuck away baskets, bins, and even drawers.

Categorizing storage

Children tend to learn about the world through categories. They first group things together by similarities, and then learn to discern the differences. (An early talker might peg all four-legged creatures as "dogs" before figuring out that some are actually "cows.") As you help children organize their belongings, you're showing them how to group objects by their function, and then divide them up into subcategories. For instance, you can point out that all toys go in the playroom, where the balls are then stored in the big basket. Kids also can see that keeping similar things together means they're easier to find – and that adding labels makes the hunt easier still.

Look for places around your home that could become storage areas. For instance, the recess beneath a staircase might house a stack of built-in drawers, each assigned a category. Atop each row, a picture and a label can lead kids to their shoes, toys, and art supplies.

Your child might like to draw or paint a picture to personalize his or her storage spaces. And it could even turn out that children involved in the process of creating good storage are also more apt to use it!

index

acknowledgments

Weldon Owen wishes to thank the following people and organizations for their generous help in producing this book

Additional photography
King Au, pages 60 (left), 148, 149, back cover (top left); Reed Davis, pages 83, 133; Paula Hible, page 92 (top right); Bill Holt, cover; David Matheson, pages 42, 53, 58 (far left), 88, 96, 97 (right), 124-25, 126-27, 130, 170-71, 175; Michael Mundy, pages 4-5; Anna Williams, page 128

Photography assistants
Tom Hood, Bill Moran, Matt Stevens

Additional styling
Kate McCann, pages 90-91, 92-93, 113, 114-15, 116-17, 138-39, 140, 145, 146, 166, 168-69

Styling assistants
Sheherazade "Shaz" Arasnia, Lolly Holloway, Greg Lowe, Renée Myers, Rob Oxenham, Melissa Scott, Meghan Wood

Photo coordinators, special projects
Brooke Lydecker, Elizabeth Russell

Merchandise coordinators
Max Baloian, Darrell Coughlan, Bryan Dobson, Scheffer Ely, Mario Serafin, Kimball Stone

Homeowners
Olivier Azancot & Natascha Couvreur, The Butti Family, Carole Chapman, John & Heather Elder, Robert Hudson & Shelly Anderson, Brian & Jennifer Kelly, Tom & Cary Nowell, Todd & Pam Severson, John & Janet Simonson, David & Ellen Turner

Design consultant
Berndt Abeck

Artworks or props
Artworks by Brendan Creemer, Emily Newell, Eloise & Georgia Shaw, and Quincy Stivers; photographs by Diane Bergren; computers from Apple Computer; magnets from Lilac Bow Yoke; Montessori products from Edu Aids

Assistance, advice, or support
Ginger Angell, Adrienne Aquino, Brett Bachtle, Leonie Barrera, Birdman Inc., Emma Boys, Tricia Burlingham & team, Nancy Chew, Peter Cieply, Kevin Crandall, Jacquelyn Dombrowski, Mara Garrity, Generations Model & Talent Agency, Emily Jahn, Kass Kapsiak (Catering by Kass), Bonnie Katz, Alissa Lillie, Rachel Lopez, Sarah Lynch, Marla Dell Talent, Meghan McDonough, Virginia McLean, Rose Meyers, Shawna Mullen, Charlie Nelson, Todd Rechner, Manny Rendon, Shadin Saah, Peter Scott, Steve's Painting & Renovating, Forrest Stilin, Police Officer Paul Stromoski, Anne Tamrazi, Sara Terrien, Jill Thompson, Richard Van Oosterhout, Scot Velardo, Angela Williams